D1199422

UNSOLVED MYSTERIES

UFOs

BY EMILY O'KEEFE

ABOUT THE AUTHOR

Emily O'Keefe is a writer and editor. She has authored many stories and lessons for children and young adults. Though she often has her head in the clouds, she has never seen a UFO. O'Keefe lives in Chicago with her cat, Chloe.

Published by The Child's World®
1980 Lookout Drive • Mankato, MN 56003-1705
800-599-READ • www.childsworld.com

ACKNOWLEDGMENTS
The Child's World®: Mary Berendes, Publishing Director
Red Line Editorial: Editorial direction
The Design Lab: Design
Amnet: Production

DESIGN ELEMENT: Shutterstock Images

PHOTOGRAPHS ©: Photobank Gallery/Shutterstock Images, Cover;
Bettmann/Corbis, 5, 8, 12; Daily Record-Union, 6; Hanns Glaser, 10;
Shell Alpert/U.S. Coast Guard/Ap Images, 15; 3Dsculptor/Istockphoto, 16;
Columbia Pictures/Album/Newscom, 19; Yiannis Papadimitriou/
Shutterstock Images, 20; George Stock, 23

ISBN 9781634070751
LCCN 2014959760

Printed in the United States of America
Mankato, MN
July, 2015
PA02266

TABLE OF CONTENTS

MYSTERIOUS SIGHTS IN THE SKY

On June 24, 1947, the weather was clear. Pilot Kenneth Arnold was flying a small plane near Mount Rainier, Washington. Suddenly, Arnold noticed a flashing light. He wondered if another plane was nearby. The pilot observed the sky carefully. He saw a plane in the distance. However, it did not have flashing lights.

Minutes later, more lights flashed near the mountain. As Arnold flew closer, he saw nine shiny aircraft. They did not look like any planes he had ever seen. Arnold measured the speed of the

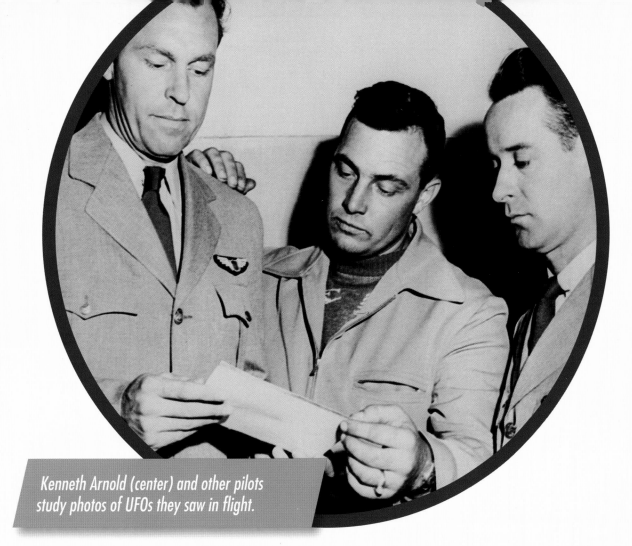

Kenneth Arnold (center) and other pilots study photos of UFOs they saw in flight.

mysterious objects. They were flying at more than 1,700 miles (2,700 km) per hour. That is faster than any known aircraft at the time.

Arnold told other pilots what he had seen. He compared the aircraft to "saucers" or round dishes. Soon, newspapers reported on the eerie "flying saucers." Readers were fascinated by Arnold's story. Some also had seen unexplained

Unidentified airships were seen over California in 1896.

objects in the sky. Scientists began to discuss these strange
sights. The experts called them unidentified flying objects,
or UFOs. What were they?

Understanding UFOs

Any object in the sky that people cannot explain can be
called a UFO. Most reported UFOs are later identified as
airplanes, strange clouds, or even bright planets. Yet some
UFOs are still mysteries.

Experts tried to explain the UFOs that Kenneth Arnold saw. Perhaps he had imagined the objects in the sky. Or he may have seen a new type of military aircraft. That could explain why the objects were so fast. Some people debated a third possibility. What if the UFOs were actually alien spaceships? **Extraterrestrials** might know how to fly very fast. They also might fly in strange aircrafts.

People had read stories about alien visitors. Movies showed imagined trips to other planets. Some Americans were excited about the idea of aliens visiting Earth. Others were frightened.

No one could fully explain Arnold's sighting. The mysterious event led to many more reports of UFOs. Another pilot spotted five or six strange flying disks in 1947. In the same year, a man said he saw a glowing creature flying a UFO.

Newspapers described more than 800 UFO sightings in 1947. Soon, the government began to study each **encounter**. Scientists tried to find explanations. Every time a UFO was reported, some people wondered if it came from outer space.

Today, people continue to see unfamiliar sights in the sky. Most are probably easy to explain. Some remain unidentified. Scientists are still looking for the answers.

Photographer Bob Jung captured a photo of one of the flying disks reported by pilots in 1947.

CHAPTER TWO

MANY YEARS OF UFO SIGHTINGS

Experts started to **investigate** UFOs in the 1940s. But people saw UFOs long before then. People have seen strange sights in the sky for hundreds of years.

In 1561 in Nuremberg, Germany, citizens saw colored globes and tubes in the sky. The shapes appeared at dawn. For hours, the shapes circled near the stars. Viewers thought the globes were attacking each other. The viewers described a battle full of light and movement. Many were frightened. Finally, the shapes

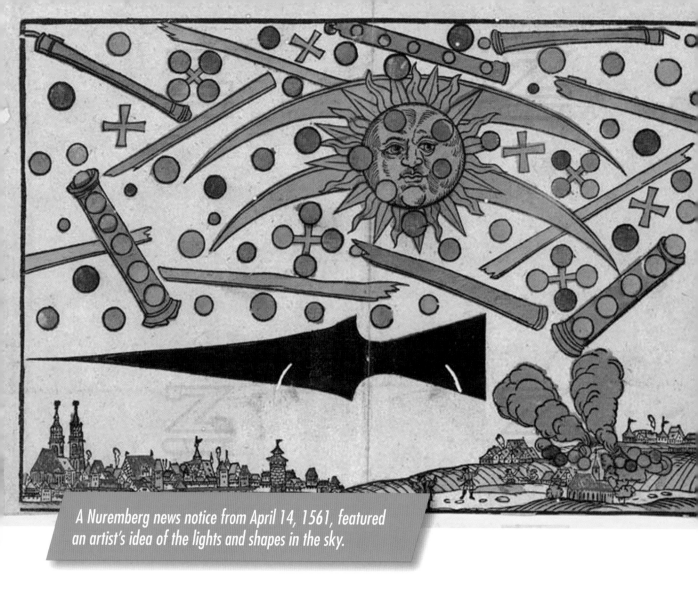

A Nuremberg news notice from April 14, 1561, featured an artist's idea of the lights and shapes in the sky.

disappeared in a cloud of smoke. No one could explain what happened.

Was this actually an alien battle? Some people think so. Dozens of witnesses described the shapes. Clearly, they saw something strange. But people in 1561 knew less about the sky than we do today. There might be a simple explanation for what they saw.

After 1561, people continued to see UFOs. Important sightings continued over the centuries. It is difficult to decide what these UFOs were. Scientists investigate by reading about the events. They check records of **phenomena** in the sky. Some unidentified objects turn out to be comets or meteors.

The Modern Age of UFOs

After airplanes were invented in the early 1900s, UFO sightings became more common. Pilots saw mysterious objects during flights. Some people mistook airplanes for UFOs. Space travel was also on people's minds. They thought more about other planets. They became interested in alien visitors to Earth.

One famous UFO sighting happened in 1947. William "Mac" Brazel was a rancher near Roswell, New Mexico. One day in July, he found **fragments** of materials on his ranch. They looked like wreckage from an air crash.

U.S. Air Force officers examine fragments of the wreckage found near Roswell in 1947.

This idea is probably a myth. A few witnesses said that they saw alien bodies near the UFO crash. They believed that the government hid the aliens. But these witnesses did not get very close to the site. The military used crash test dummies to test the safety of their vehicles. Most likely, the witnesses saw these dummies.

Brazel had seen news reports about flying disks. He wondered if the materials were from a crashed saucer. U.S. Air Force officials studied the wreckage. At first, they could not identify it. Finally, they decided that a **weather balloon** had crashed.

Other people disagreed. Reporters talked to Brazel's neighbors. One had seen a strange aircraft before the crash. A few people later claimed that they saw aliens at the crash site.

For years, debates about Roswell continued. In 1994, the U.S. Air Force shared new information. They said that the wreckage was from a military vehicle. It had been part of a secret project. Officials at the time were not allowed to say what it really was.

Most scientists believe this explanation. They say the Roswell case has been solved. Yet many Americans think that aliens were in Roswell. Every year, people visit the city. Some are still looking for clues.

CHAPTER THREE

FINDING THE TRUTH

After Roswell, people wondered if UFOs were dangerous. The government decided to investigate.

In 1947, Project Blue Book began. This program tracked UFO sightings for 22 years. Officials studied approximately 12,600 reports of UFOs. They gathered evidence about each case. They found explanations for most sightings. However, 701 of the cases remain unsolved.

Project Blue Book ended in 1969. The government decided that UFOs were not a threat.

A U.S. Coast Guard photographer snapped this picture of bright lights in the sky near Salem, Massachusetts, on July 16, 1952.

Many **ufologists** still wanted answers. They formed groups to study UFOs. Some still track sightings around the world. The National UFO Reporting Center records hundreds of sightings every month.

Fast-moving satellites are often mistaken for UFOs.

How do these experts investigate? First, they speak to people who saw the UFO. They find out what it looked like. Experts look for **reliable** witnesses. For example, pilots know a lot about airplanes and the sky. Often, they can help solve the case.

Then, experts look for other evidence. This evidence can include photographs and aircraft wreckage. Last, the investigators think carefully about the evidence. They decide on the most likely explanation. If the experts are sure, the object is identified. If they are not sure, it remains unidentified.

MYTH OR FACT?
Most UFO sightings happen in small towns.

This is a fact. Most UFO sightings happen in small towns or farm areas. Some people see UFOs in cities. However, city buildings can block lights in the sky. People in small towns have a better view of the stars. They are more likely to see UFOs in the sky.

CHAPTER FOUR

UFOs TODAY

UFO sightings remain common. One in seven Americans says he or she has seen a UFO. Experts have learned a lot about this mystery, but they still have questions. Are some UFOs from outer space? No one can say for sure.

Some scientists doubt that any UFOs are from space. The scientists say that if aliens were here, they would leave more clues. Often, the only evidence of UFOs is from witnesses' stories. There are few clear photographs. No alien spaceships have been recovered.

It would also be difficult for aliens to travel to Earth. If there is life on other planets, that life is very far away. It could take aliens thousands of years to reach Earth. The trip might be impossible.

However, aliens may travel in ways we do not understand. Some people say that there is no other explanation for certain UFO cases. Others are unsure. They want to see more evidence before they decide.

Recent UFO Mysteries

One recent UFO sighting happened in Stephenville, Texas. A pilot was at a campfire. He saw a beautiful, glowing light. At first, he thought it was the sunset. Then he noticed that the light was flashing. It seemed like the light was coming from a large object in the sky. This object moved silently but quickly. There were lights all around it.

Many amateur astronomers use telescopes to search the night sky for UFOs.

UFO experts arrived in the town. They knew it was an important sighting. Dozens of people had seen the mysterious aircraft. Many believed that something unusual was in the sky. Reporters found possible explanations. Perhaps the UFO was an **illusion**. People might have seen two airplanes. Sunlight reflections could make them look like one object. That would explain why the object looked so big. Fighter jets had also been flying in the area. People might have seen flares from the jets. Some witnesses did not believe these explanations. They said that the object looked different from anything they had seen.

Still, there is little **documentation** for most UFOs. This is why the mystery is so difficult to solve. New technology could fix this problem. People can track UFOs online. Many people now carry cameras with them. These tools may help gather the evidence to find out what UFOs really are.

MYTH OR FACT?
People have only seen UFOs in the United States.

This idea is a myth. Most UFO sightings happen in the United States. Yet people have also seen UFOs in other places. Sightings have been reported in Canada, Japan, the United Kingdom, and other countries. In Brazil, thousands of people saw a UFO in June 2013.

Glossary

aerial (AIR-ee-uhl) Something aerial is happening in the air. UFOs are aerial objects.

documentation (dok-yuh-men-TAY-shun) Documentation is official evidence or information. Documentation of UFOs includes written reports, photographs, and videos.

encounter (en-KOUN-tur) An encounter is an unexpected meeting with a person or thing. Many Americans believe they have had an encounter with a UFO.

extraterrestrials (ek-struh-tuh-RES-tree-uhlz) Extraterrestrials are creatures from other planets. Some people think that extraterrestrials come to Earth in UFOs.

fragments (FRAG-muhnts) Fragments are small pieces broken off of a larger object. Scientists study fragments of UFOs to identify them.

illusion (ih-LOO-zhun) An illusion is something that people believe they see but is not really there. Some people think the Stephenville UFO was an illusion.

investigate (in-VES-tuh-gayt) People investigate by looking for clues to solve a mystery. Experts may investigate a UFO by talking to people who reported seeing it.

phenomena (fe-NAH-muh-nuh) Phenomena are unusual facts or events that scientists study. UFOs are unexplained phenomena in the sky.

reliable (ri-LYE-uh-buhl) A reliable person or thing is honest and trustworthy. UFO experts speak to witnesses who give reliable reports of what they saw.

ufologists (yoo-EFF-ah-low-jists) Ufologists are people who study UFOs. Each time an important UFO sighting occurs, ufologists study the evidence.

weather balloon (WETH-ur buh-LOON) A weather balloon is a hot-air balloon used to gather information about the weather. Officials stated that the UFO was a weather balloon.

To Learn More

BOOKS

Duncan, John. *The Unexplained: UFOs.* Milwaukee, WI: Gareth Stevens, 2005.

Jeffrey, Gary. *UFOs: Alien Abduction and Close Encounters.* New York: Rosen, 2006.

Perish, Patrick. *Are UFOs Real?* Mankato, MN: Amicus, 2013.

WEB SITES

Visit our Web site for links about UFOs: **childsworld.com/links**

Note to Parents, Teachers, and Librarians: We routinely verify our Web links to make sure they are safe and active sites. So encourage your readers to check them out!

Index